Basics Before Buzz

MANAGING IN CHALLENGING TIMES

Kevin Kelly

Acknowledgements

Thanks to:

My Editor and friend, Eileen Bennett and committed agent, Ita O Driscoll for their tireless work on this Project.

My expert review group that constructively dissected the initial drafts – Pat Byrne, (Department Manager of Enterprise Ireland's High Potential Start ups), Dr. James Cunningham, (School of Business & Economics National University of Ireland, Galway), Martin Corry, (Enterprise Ireland), Gary Loughlin, (Entrepreneur), Gary Allen, (Nortel), Brendan Deeney, (Training Manager),Michelle Bailly, (Consultant) and Fergal McAndrew.

Cathal Divilly MD of Great Place to Work Institute Ireland for his superb contribution.

Anna Maria Newell for her microscopic proof reading.

My parents Kevin and Mary Kelly, a constant source of inspiration in my life.

My friends who continue to support and inspire me.

Deirdre for her patience, love, advice, sense of fun and friendship right throughout this rather extended journey!

Dedicated to Conor, my fearless, determined,
happy bundle of unconditional love.

Introduction

Of course you're busy!

As a Manager or a Business Owner or an Entrepreneur, you may say you have enough problems at the moment making ends meet without investing valuable time and money in a book. The question is can you afford not to read it?

Maybe you won't be impressed by the amount of recent research and the in-depth studies I have collected to support the information between these pages?

Maybe you don't care that Great Places to Work Ireland interviewed over 30,000 employees and have shared the insights gleaned from that body of work with me?

Maybe you don't think you've anything to learn?

But get this:

The 'Boss' no longer exists

The 'Job' no longer exists

'Business as usual' no longer exists.

Every business is fundamentally about people - your

Time to Move on!

customers, your employees and you. This book explores those three key areas and tells you how best to maximise the potential of each.

The first section will reveal how predictable your customers are and how you can use this knowledge to deliver an exceptional service. Exceptional service is a necessary pre-requisite for customer retention in the current environment.

The next section deals with your employees – your internal customers – and shows you how to unleash their natural creativity, keep them motivated in uncertain times and help them reach their full potential.

And the third section is about where it all begins, with you.

Of course, whatever applies to your customers equally applies to your employees and to you; so the insights you glean from each section can be used in every interaction.

Stanford Business School Advisory Board, reports that self-awareness has been recognised as the most important capability for leaders to develop.

Until you know yourself, and what motivates and inspires you, you cannot motivate or inspire anybody else.

And let's face it, if you're not motivating and inspiring your staff, how can you expect them to motivate or inspire your customers to buy your product or service?

And if your staff is not enticing your customers to buy your product or service again and again, you don't have a business!

So, forget all the buzz and hype you've ever heard about what makes business work well, and get right back to basics!

Table of Contents

Customers Are Predictable

It is good news that there are certain sure-fire assumptions you can make about the people who buy your products or service!

Customers crave and thrive on positive attention!

Customers are overwhelmed.

Customers like people who are like themselves.

Customers cannot lie successfully.

It's even better news that, once you are familiar with these assumptions, you can use them to deliver such outstanding service that your customers will become loyal friends.

In this section, we will explore in depth each of these core assumptions and how they can give you a real edge over your competitors.

Assumption 1
Customers crave and thrive on positive attention!

I was commissioned to do a training session with a group of fifty people who worked for a multinational company. Even before I was introduced, a man shouted out from the back of the group "when is this going to be over?"

Not a great start, I thought!

Since his interjection had raised a question in everyone's mind, I began by telling the audience when I expected the session to finish. I then addressed my impatient friend and asked his name.

'John' he said.

I spoke directly to him.

'John, imagine that you are interviewing me for a sales job. I want you and the audience to assess me before I even open my mouth. Analyse how I walk into the imaginary interview room and so on.'

I walked down to the back of the room and gave John a strong, confident handshake and went back to the podium.

'Ok' I said, addressing the whole room 'just remember that John is interviewing me for a sales job. His task and yours is to assess me on your first impressions.'

Down I went again to John and shook his hand before returning to the podium.

After the third time, walking down to where John was sitting and shaking his hand, I asked him for his opinion on my approach.

A few minutes later, directing my attention away from him, I said 'as John mentioned earlier' and repeated the most relevant comment he had made.

By now there was a major shift in John's body language. He was sitting forward with his eyes firmly fixed on me. John had moved from being a big challenge in a learning environment to, at the very least, being neutral.

By addressing John's "challenging behaviour," using his name and including him in the learning process, I was giving him attention and satisfying his need to be appreciated.

Another great rapport builder is repeating back to people what they have said. When you repeat people's words back to them, you are not only showing you are listening, you are also attaching importance to their words. When I – the perceived expert in this situation – referred the audience to John's comments, I was validating his input and helping him feel good about himself.

What happens when a trainer moves around a room? Usually the audience follows him/her with their eyes. When I went down to John on the three occasions the whole audience was feeding him attention at a subconscious level and he revelled in it. Attention works.

The handshakes also had an impact because shaking hands helps to establish connection and build rapport.

You will find many 'Johns' among your employees and customer base. They crave for and demand attention.

How Do You Raise Your Game to Meet Your Clients' Needs?

Start by imagining that you are about to lose every single customer, one by one. For some businesses there is no need to imagine, the exodus has started already.

Constructive Paranoia

So what can you do to keep them? What changes can you make in the way you treat them? How can you persuade them to stay?

This exercise in Constructive Paranoia is really valuable for helping you identify what you can do better.

Make those moments count!

Your starting point is to forensically examine every point of contact between your customers and the organisation and to focus on exceeding expectations at every opportunity.

> **NEWS**
>
> One Bain and Co survey found that every four years a company loses 50% of its customers.
>
> The average business never hears from 96% of its unhappy customers and it costs five times more to attract a new client as opposed to servicing an existing one.
>
> (Research compiled by Technical Assistance Research Programme, U.S.A.)

Customer Retention

WHY?

- Research has shown that a 5% decrease in defections can improve a firm's bottom line by 25% and upwards, so get your customer's fault finding!

- An unhappy customer whose complaint was satisfactorily resolved will tell up to five people about the positive treatment they received.

- Loyal shoppers tend to spend four times as much in their favourite store as opposed to promiscuous shoppers. (Research by Technical Assistance Research Programme, U.S.A.)

Manage All Contact Points

HOW?

A great example of this forensic attention to detail comes from Disneyworld who decided to make the lettering on the shampoo and conditioner bottles bigger because they thought people found it difficult to read them in the shower

They also put good reading lights (with higher watt bulbs than standard) in their hotel rooms beside the beds to make it more comfortable to read.

This type of detailed analysis creates a better, more memorable experience for the customer.

But you don't need to be a huge corporation like Disney to make a real impact on your customers and keep them coming back. Most of this book was written on my laptop in the little coffee shop near my home. Every time I walk through the door I am greeted by name and made to feel welcome. I normally don't have to open my mouth before my order arrives quickly and with a smile.

That's why I go back there again and again. It's like a home from home!

Every organisation - small or large – can set high standards and create policies around how customers are treated. For instance: how quickly are people dealt with when they walk into the reception area or what is the accepted lead time between a telephone enquiry and the delivery of promotional information/materials?

There is always room for improvement!

There are many opportunities to help strengthen the customer bond that are not currently being exploited:

TAKE ACTION!

Get a page and list every possible area where customers connect with your business. Think about every point of contact.

Now set standards for each in conjunction with your team. The philosophy then should be to exceed the customer's expectations at every one of these points of contact.

Solicit and Solve Complaints

Complaints represent a unique opportunity to strengthen relationship with your customers! The fact is that most people don't expect complaints to be handled well, so when you train your team to detonate this potential time bomb at base, you immediately exceed your customer's expectations.

Of course, there is a right and wrong way of dealing with complaints.

Shoes Without Sole!

Some time back I purchased a pair of shoes. Two days later the shoes were making their debut in the auspicious surroundings of the Grimaldi Forum in Monaco. Just before I entered the conference room the sole of one shoe detached itself. Thankfully I was happy to remove my shoes, turn the crisis into a comedy and address the audience in my socks!

When I got home I revisited the shop where the shoes had been purchased, approached the customer service staff and explained the situation.

After reviewing the shoes and the receipt, she indicated that she would have to speak with the manager!!

I was left standing at the top of a growing queue while she discussed my case with her superior before eventually refunding the price of the shoes!

There was only one acceptable way of dealing with this situation:

a sincere apology followed by a refund on the spot. Nobody needs a further cross-examination or an induced feeling of guilt as your case is thrashed out in front of other customers.

I greatly admire companies who choose to take the rap over seemingly 'unreasonable' complaints. Their research has shown that this response positively affects the bottom line.

Top companies empower employees to respond at the contact point wherever possible. For example: the Ritz-Carlton hotel chain authorises their employees to deal with any problem at source and to implement or create any customer satisfaction solution that will cost under $2,000.

If the scale of the complaint means that the employee needs to seek counsel with a superior, communication is key. The customer must be kept informed, given a detailed timeline and be told when they can expect a resolution of the issue. Then the challenge is to execute the planned resolution even more efficiently so that you really start building bridges!

I believe that we need to do better than merely solving complaints. We need to be proactive at eliciting them. Remember, 96% of dissatisfied people never complain to you directly but leave anyway! (Source: Technical Assistance Research Programme, U.S.A.) In addition to organising focus groups and regular customer surveys you need to be more immediate in your strategy – elicit complaints at interface. This needs to be a lot more than the programmed, canned "did you enjoy your meal" routine.

Get them complaining!

We need to engage in what I describe as reverse selling:
extract complaints and ideas from your customers and integrate
this feedback into a new product offering — then sell your target
audience back 'their' product. The customer now has an aspect of
ownership in the product and will be much more inclined to buy it.
This was the strategy I successfully employed to dramatically increase
the turnover in many of the companies I worked for, before setting
up my own marketing consultancy in 1990.

Guarantee Your Service

If you want to go one step further, design a customer charter with your team that guarantees the levels of service your customer can expect at each contact point. For your customer, this takes away the risk of buying from you and sends a very clear message to the market: you mean business and you have total confidence in your product or service and the people who deliver it.

Ultimately in a way you need to be able to 'dunk' your customers; by this I mean, send them to the competition in the knowledge that they would never defect.

Dunkin Donuts – 'the world's largest coffee and baked goods chain' - paid some of their loyal customers €100 a week to buy their coffee at Starbucks instead, and paid Starbucks customers a similar amount to make the switch to them.

Both focus groups decided to remain loyal to their original choice.

Are you confident enough in your product or service to send your customers off to the competition?

If the thought strikes fear in your heart, you need to start reviewing your value proposition.

Convert Customers To Friends

Overall, in this new business world you have to Think Differently. Think outside the box and see how you can exceed expectations and retain loyalty.

So what could you do for your clients outside of the traditional relationship?

Can you secure business for them? Suggest different product ideas for their mix? Send them through competitor information?

Conversion the key

When you exceed customer's expectations you start to build a more authentic relationship with clients which moves them closer to a more sustainable business model, i.e. customers become your friends. Remember, customers leave; friends don't.

Focus on converting your customers into friends.

Team Effort

In Africa there is a saying, 'it takes a village to raise a child'. In the current business environment, it takes a company to keep a client. The conversion process is everyone's business and not just the domain of the Customer Service Department.

Great View

Cut out the middle man

Often when something goes wrong and client expectations are not met, the breakdown is actually not between the client and the sales person (or the custodian of the relationship) but actually between the client and the support/office/admin staff. In many cases - because they don't deal with the client face to face - the support staff are not aware of clients' expectations, needs or wants,

One innovative company noticed this and as a result, at certain times during the year, sent the support staff on the road with the sales person to visit clients face to face. First hand they got a grip on the wants and expectations of the client. This made the whole process of client expectation to client delivery seamless.

Support staff feel a greater sense of involvement in the company's bottom line, it improves teamwork between sales and support and the client is happy as they get what they paid for.

Cathal Divilly www.greatplacetowork.ie

Assumption 2
Customers Like People Who Are Like Themselves

In the context of building rapport, there is no doubt that the more we mirror people's behaviour, body language, tone of voice etc, the more they begin to like us.

All you need to do is to watch two people in agreement from a distance and you will notice that they subconsciously mirror each other. From folding arms to crossing legs to moving their hands, they unconsciously perform an intimate mirroring dance.

A study published by Ulf Dimberg of the University of Uppsala, Sweden, has shown that our natural tendency is to mirror other human beings.

He discovered that when volunteers were asked to mirror certain facial expressions, the task was completed with effortless ease.

When on the other hand, the volunteers were asked to mismatch or provide the opposite expression to what they were seeing, for example, to frown when the other person was smiling, their muscles continued to try to produce a smile.

The ability to mirror, to walk in someone shoes, is a fantastic rapport tool and appears to be a natural ability, if we allow it to flow!

By observing my audience during a seminar, I can always

tell which people will end up together at the break. They may be sitting at opposite ends of the room and they may never have met before, but I can guarantee that the people whose body language is transmitting negative feedback will all find each other over coffee and have a good moan!

Similarly, the people who have been enjoying the seminar will locate a kindred spirit, because, at a subconscious level, we all seek out energies that match our own.

In summary your focus must be very much on walking a mile in your customer's moccasins, as the old Indian saying goes.

We communicate via our body language, voice projection and words – beware of the following mirroring challenges!

Don't turn up in a farmer's yard wearing a designer suit!

Don't speak at hundred miles an hour to a customer who speaks in a slow monotone voice.

Don't speak like a dictator to an interviewer or anyone with a nervous disposition!

At a technical level, don't forget to speak their language:

People invariably communicate in one of three styles:

Visual = lots of gestures. Will say things like 'I see…' or 'Look at this…' so in a sales pitch SHOWING THEM pictures, brochures, press coverage will have a lot of impact.

Auditory = learn by listening and need clear verbal instructions. Like detail. Will listen intently to your words and use phrases such as 'Sounds good…' or 'Rings a bell…' so TELL THEM stories, talk them through your selling points and so on.

Kinaesthetic = need to feel how something works. Very hands on and use phrases like 'I sense…' or 'That feels right…' so CREATE AN EXPERIENCE, give them a demonstration so they can get a grasp on your subject and so on.

Making an oral presentation to Mrs Visual may not be the best way forward! The most effective communicators can seamlessly weave a picture, a story and a feeling into the same presentation so that everybody gets the message.

Assumption 3
Customers are overwhelmed

Message Bombardment

In the 1970's the average city dweller was exposed to 500 to 2,000 ad messages a day; today it's between 3,000 and 5,000. (Yankelovich, October 2006)

We are each being bombarded with up to 5,000 marketing messages every day – and that's on top of having to deal with work-related and personal phone calls, emails, text messages, letters, conversations and the myriad of other ways we are being targeted for attention.

Not only are we overwhelmed we are distracted!

Have you noticed the huge shift from conversation to presentation, and from dialogue to monologue? Check this pattern out today. Observe how few real conversations take place and that there are more and more presentations. Honouring their insatiable appetite for attention, people look like they are going to pounce on their colleagues as they wait to either interrupt or 'present' their contribution!

Jay Conrad Levinson, the father of guerrilla marketing, highlights research that shows that a person must be exposed to an advert 27 times before they are ready to take action.

In this environment, you've got to be different to be noticed!

Know Your Business and Your Message

Selling is everyone's challenge and one prerequisite for success is that every employee knows what business you're in and can communicate that in a meaningful way. For example, all Medtronic employees know that 'every 4 seconds, the life of someone, somewhere in the world is improved by a Medtronic product or therapy.'

So, every Medtronic employee is in no doubt that what he or she does at work every day makes a real, positive difference.

> *"Every leader needs to clearly explain the top three things the organisation is working on. If you can't, then you're not leading well."*
>
> GE's Jeff Immelt

Of course as has been said many, many times before; you can't expect people to travel with you if they don't know where they are going.

Package That Message: Make It An Experience

In The Future of Competition (Harvard Business School Press, 2004), University of Michigan professor C.K. Prahalad emphasises 'Experience is the brand.'

To stand out from the crowd and catch (and hold) your customer's over-stimulated attention you have to attach a memorable experience to the product or service.

Sony Style, the 12,000 sq ft Sony flagship store in Hong Kong, is divided into various zones where customers are encouraged to try the products. The Home Theatre zone, for example, looks like an average living room and allows the customer to sit on the sofa and imagine how the products would look and sound in their own home.

Adidas stores provide running tracks where people can have a real experience of the shoes before buying them. Their new 3000 sq ft signature store in Beijing will push the brand boundaries and be the first to pioneer fully integrated sports and lifestyle solutions via experiential options like different virtual features centred on the core skills of sports which will help customers in their favourite sports. The store will also feature a wide menu of services targeted at providing an holistic platform for sports and sport lifestyle such as professional running clinics, in-house fitness coaches, style advisors etc.

Being 'as good as' the rest doesn't register in the customer's memory in today's busy, noisy and demanding world.

My own training style acknowledges the fact that we are living in an Attention Deficit Society and that the average listening span is approximately 15 minutes. So, in any presentation that lasts for 60 minutes I will engage the audience in various exercises at least 4 times. I would also ensure that everyone was getting the full experience by using different styles of presentation: visual, auditory and kinaesthetic.

People buy into and remember emotion, but are rarely moved by cold facts.

Tell Them Stories

If you want to get your message across and avoid their conscious filtering system; tell them stories. They can't resist. People love and remember stories.

Use stories about happy clients, positive experiences, problems solved or how you integrated ideas from feedback and improved the product or service.

Be Brief!

Thus when pitching you must be brief. For example if it was a new sales presentation, I believe you should be able to pitch yourself in two minutes flat, and more critically you have to capture the imagination in that 120 seconds.

And, if all else fails, as mentioned before, just listen.

Ask your customers questions, let them speak and really listen to what they have to say.

Remember, you are giving them their favourite drug: attention!

I recall some years back visiting a potential client with a sales trainee. From the moment we said our hello's it was obvious that the client loved to talk and the normal sales presentation was not going to happen in this instance. So every now and again I would interject and ask the customer a question that included one of my client's selling points. So for example I asked "How important is it to you Mark that the company you deal with is the leading manufacturer in the marketplace?" Mark answered and continued his presentation! Approximately thirty minutes later after interjecting three times we decided we had to leave. The sales trainee opened his mouth for the first time and asked for the order and Mark, buoyed by our time together, agreed. Deal done!

Assumption 4
Customers cannot lie successfully

An intimate connection exists between our physiology (the way we look) and our psychology (the way we think), so if you want to know whether someone is bored or exhilarated, a quick scan of their physiology will give you the answer.

Indeed sometimes a person's words may say 'yes' but it will be crystal clear from their body language - poor eye contact, a change in posture or voice projection etc - that what they really meant to say was 'no'. Words just got in the way!

Some time back I was a member of a panel interviewing people for a sales position. One particular candidate strode confidently into the room, pulled the chair right up to the table and placed his hands no more than a couple of inches away from mine and my colleagues.

How would you react to this?

When a stranger invades your personal space like that your first reaction is to withdraw, because at a subconscious level, you interpret this behaviour as an act of aggression.

His actions immediately put the entire interview panel into defence mode!

In the course of the interview, it emerged that this candidate had started a company that had failed. Even after careful questioning he was not prepared to take any responsibility for this failure and blamed other people, the economy, market forces and his competitors for his lack of success.

This spoke volumes to me and the other panel members and confirmed our first impression; this was an arrogant man and not suited to the position.

A person's physiology rarely lies.

Thus, you should pay more attention to body language - posture, gestures, the way people walk, blood circulation in their face, breathing patterns, voice projection - than you do to what a person says.

The information you glean from this analysis will dictate whether or not you should persist or leave the negotiating table. If I notice any consistent negative body language during a negotiation, regardless of whether or not it has taken weeks to get to meet the person, I immediately honour this and offer to leave. This strategy has had a major positive effect on my sales figures.

After noticing negative body language I normally will say "Dave/Mary/Madam President, I can see you have other things on your mind. Maybe we can leave it for now and reschedule at a better time for you in the future?"

There are a few possible outcomes (all positive):

The client apologises for their lack of attention and starts to focus on the negotiations – this is usually a good sign that a sale is imminent.

The client agrees to a reschedule in the future. This means that unlike many, many salespeople who persist regardless of the client's non-verbal feedback, the door is open to future negotiations.

The client is impressed by your exit strategy and precipitates positive word of mouth within his business circles.

Communication, it is definitely far more than words.

When you meet someone for the first time, 55% of your decision on whether or not you like them is based on their body language, 38% on their voice projection, and just 7% on the words they use.

So how long does it take to form that all-powerful first impression? Research completed by Harvard psychology professors Nalini Ambady, Ph.D., and Robert Rosenthal, Ph.D. confirmed our deepest suspicions - the time you've got to make an impact is reducing!

"Observers viewed three thin slices of each professor's behaviour – in 10-second clips from the beginning, middle and end of a class - and then rated the professors' confidence, energy and warmth. They found that these ratings predicted with amazing accuracy the average student rating taken at semester's end. Thinner slices - three two-second clips - also yielded ratings similarly congruent with student evaluations."

A researcher from NYU claims the time is even faster!

"We're finding that everything is evaluated as good or bad within a quarter of a second," says John A. Bargh.

To check how good you are at interpreting body language, try muting the sound on your favourite television program and see how well you can decipher what's going on!

In a Nutshell

People Are Predictable

Raise your game to meet your customer's needs and improve customer retention by;

- Managing all contact points
- Soliciting and solving complaints
- Guaranteeing your service
- Thinking and doing differently
- Using team effort

Capture your customer's imagination by:

- Knowing your business and your message
- Packaging that message: make it an experience
- Telling them stories
- Being brief

Overall businesses need to exceed customers' expectations if they expect to retain their key customers.

Creative Potential

So now you know that your customers exhibit predictable behaviours and how you can use these facts to your advantage.

This section will explore how you can tap into the creative potential of your employees – your internal customer - to maximum effect.

More and more companies are finding that product life cycles are decreasing so it is critically important to have a flow of ideas that become the new generation of products for your organisation.

The lines of demarcation between the various sections in any organisation are becoming blurred. Forward-thinking companies have long recognised that every member of staff is actually a sales person. But what if every member of staff was also part of the Creative Team? How would your business change if every employee's job description stipulated that they contribute one idea a month on how any aspect of their job could be improved?

To back up this initiative it would be imperative that a structure is in place to both harvest and develop the contributions. There is potential for a new role in an organisation - Ideas executive?

In late 2007, Phillips invited all 125,000 of its workers around the world to stop working and focus on thinking of ways to simplify the processes. The best ideas to come from this experiment would be implemented in all Phillips factories worldwide. This type of initiative would be a major internal Public Relations disaster if an implementation plan wasn't in place.

Remember, even minor improvements over time can turn into a revolution, as asserted by Katsuaki Watanabe, Toyota President.

'There is no genius in our company. We just do whatever we

believe is right, trying every day to improve every little bit and piece, but when 70 years of very small improvements accumulate, they become a revolution.'

Having overtaken General Motors, Toyota is now the largest car manufacturer in the world.

Another interesting piece of research highlights the importance of not overlooking the ordinary and on focusing continually on the extraordinary in the context of innovation. Professor Amar Bhide of Columbia University found that only 12% of growth company founders attribute their success to an unusual or extraordinary idea while 88% reported that their success was due to "exceptional execution of an ordinary idea."

Einstein once said that you cannot solve problems with the level of thinking that created them. He also said that the definition of insanity is to keep doing the same thing over and over again expecting a different result! And he also said that imagination is more important than knowledge!

So, change your thinking and move from the way 'things have always been done' and you'll get a different outcome. It is important that individuals are allowed the freedom to act and think differently.

To kick-start creativity in the workplace here is my 13-Step Program

- Trust them

- Keep them informed

- Invest in them

- Engage them in a meaningful way

- Give them more than money

- Exceed their expectations

- Cultivate community

- Recruit right!

- Ask

- Model off the creative mind

- Show your staff how to switch off

- Trust wisdom over knowledge

- Value feedback over failure

Trust – The Cornerstone

The starting point of any strategy to unleash creativity within the workplace must be to establish trust and truly engage your most intangible asset. Engagement is the route to developing a high-trust culture. This is the challenge for the organisation of tomorrow, especially in the light of recent research!

In a study conducted by Watson Wyatt across ten European countries, 35 - 41% of people were considering leaving their employment. Forty one percent of Irish respondents were in this space.

Further evidence from recent studies suggests that only 30% of employees are actively "engaged" in their jobs and one in five are positively disengaged. (Gallup Q12 Benchmarking Survey). In 2004 Gallup estimated that there were 22 million people in the workplace but not actually working, costing the US economy up to $300 billion annually in lost productivity alone.

Worse still some of them are asleep!

According to a survey conducted in 2006 by Monster Ireland, one third of respondents admitted to falling asleep on the job with another 35% saying they found it a big challenge to keep awake.

These results show that, not only is absenteeism an issue today, 'presenteeism' is also a key challenge.

Meanwhile extensive research carried out by Towers Perrin has shown engagement has a positive effect on the bottom line and in retaining staff – no surprises here!

GREAT VIEW

Employee engagement should take place as part of a structured plan where management is 100% clear on what they are trying to achieve by soliciting the opinions of employees. It should take place using a strict methodology at a set time during the year and there must be commitment from senior management to follow up on the outcomes.

There are also dangers when it comes to employee engagement. Unless there is follow through on the outcomes it can really damage management integrity and act as a serious demotivator for all involved.

It's very important to be aware that the agenda is not about introducing best practices because they are the latest buzzword or the latest people practice topic. Any new initiatives must make sense for your organisation. This is why the starting point is to know the demographics of your organisation. Ask questions like:

How many female/male employees do we have?

What is the age profile of our organisation?

How many of our employees have children?

It is important to be able to answer these questions because people from different demographics expect and are motivated by different things.

For example, after engaging with their employees, one company realised they had some issues in the area of work-life balance. They decided that 'work-life balance' meant family friendly initiatives and without considering their employee demographics spent a lot of money on introducing schemes that catered for employees with families.

Follow-on engagement with their employees revealed that work-life balance was still an area they struggled with because over 60% of their organisation did not have families, so the new family friendly initiatives did not appeal to them at all and had actually isolated most of the workforce.

Know your demographic profiles before you introduce new people practices and initiatives.

Cathal Divilly www.greatplacetowork.ie

Keep Them Informed

Communication is key. In the new organisation, two-way feedback - a 360 degree process should be in place so owners/entrepreneurs and not just "employees" are evaluated.

At Dell, all the management team including Michael Dell are rated by their subordinates in 'Tell Dell' surveys. Furthermore, a manager who is not addressing the employee's issues, will not be promoted. If your score is low all the time, question marks will be placed over your suitability for the job.

The evaluation of Nokia's top two hundred executives depends on how their subordinates rate their ability to lead, teach and inspire.

At Price Waterhouse Cooper Ireland their Peer and Upward feedback scheme allows employees to provide anonymous feedback about the people they work with.

People not only benefit from regular feedback but are also affirmed in that their opinion is valued by other team members.

Transparency and trust are the lifeblood of the new organisation.

GREAT VIEW

Communication is not about passing on only the good news or issuing 'top down' statements. It is about developing a comprehensive communication program that ensures that all your organisation hear the message and have an available mechanism to deliver a message to management.

The best companies will have an array of communication mechanisms at their disposal that brings all organisation demographics into the communication program. They will not only deliver good news but also the bad news. Timely communication of bad news will stop the need for a rumour mill, which is a very unhealthy way for information to be spread.

Cathal Divilly www.greatplacetowork.ie

People should be positively affirmed on their current performance and given a roadmap, and the tools to help them overcome any challenges highlighted.

The old and tired concern that if you give too much praise, people may get 'above their station' or 'big-headed' is well past its sell by date.

Praise, like gold and diamonds, owes its value only to its scarcity.

Samuel Beckett

In recessionary times, keeping the information flowing is imperative. In its absence, a misinformed grapevine that induces fear within the workplace oftentimes takes over. This fear has a negative effect on motivation levels, productivity and creativity.

Invest in Them

There should be an ongoing focus on developing talent. This strategy should be immune to the ups and downs in the marketplace. Too often Training and Development is cut whenever markets recede.

GREAT VIEW

The companies that get the area of Training and Development correct are those that have a clear link between the T&D on offer and a transparent promotional process. Employees need to feel rewarded through promotions as a result of partaking in developmental courses.

The Best Companies are aware that each employee has two lives - a personal life and a professional life - and will offer personal developmental courses as well as professional courses. The business sense is that if you can motivate and assist an employee to pursue their personal interests they will be a better rounded more motivated professional.

Cathal Divilly www.greatplacetowork.ie

At American Express 25% of an executive's variable pay depends on talent development.

Also the company's 12-member executive board meets four to five times with protégés at Vice President level during a six-month program.

Have you ever considered rotating your managers between the various departments or divisions of your organisation to broaden their insights and provide experience in a wide range of different roles?

Engage Them In A Meaningful Way

Sam Palmisano, CEO of IBM obviously understood
this when he initiated a company wide online process
in which all employees around the globe had the
opportunity to participate for three days in determining
what IBM's values should be.

Steve Jobs, the co-founder of Apple Computer, said,
"The only thing that works is management by values. Find people
who are competent and really bright, but more importantly, people
who care exactly about the same things you care about."

Furthermore, living the company values should be recognised
and affirmed on an ongoing basis. Values are something we invest
time, energy and resources in. There is little point in saying you value
your people if no communication has taken place with staff in weeks!

Share values!

Values that Endure - Musgrave story

One of the indicators of a great place to work is when you can select anyone at random from the floor and elicit positive feedback. Recently I met an assembly operative who voluntarily enthused about his first year working for Musgraves in Ireland.

Musgraves was founded in 1876 by brothers Stuart and Thomas Musgrave. The company is now one of the top five grocery retailers and partners to food retailers in the British Isles employing more than 5,500 and with a turnover of €4.9bn in 2007. Staff retention is high; a large number of employees have been with the company for over thirty years. In 2007 Musgraves were the first Irish indigenous company to win the Chamber of Irelands President's Award for the Overall Outstanding Achievement in Corporate Social Responsibility.

Noel, who was previously self-employed, joined Musgraves on the recommendation of an existing staff member. He is now working shifts and enjoying being with a company that "keeps you informed of all happenings within the organisation, provides training opportunities to allow you up-skill (at the moment he is doing the EXCEL computer course), gives you the potential to be upwardly mobile within the organisation and looks after you financially by giving you great opportunities to make a decent living".

In his first year, Noel has already become a great ambassador for his company and, like his work colleagues, expects to be there for years to come.

How do you inspire such loyalty from an employee?

*According to Sandra Looney, Group HR Manager, one
of the core reasons for Musgrave's extraordinary success is their
strong foundation i.e. their core values. Their five values
- long-term stable relationships, honesty, working hard,
achievement and not being greedy - permeate and underpin
everything they do.*

*"Our values define how we work with our partners
(suppliers, retailers, employees). For example, at recruitment
level, finding the person who fits the organisation and the
behaviours associated with the values is as important as the
skills match. While working at Musgraves it is critical that
employees demonstrate that they live the Musgraves values.
This is assessed on an annual basis as part of our engagement
survey. The values of the top 220 managers across the group
are assessed using a 360-degree tool.*

*Noel is a living embodiment of the Musgraves values.
His positive relationship with the organisation is based on
transparency, trust and respect. He knows we are willing to
invest in him and work to maximize his potential within the
organisation. The important role he plays and commitment
he shows is rewarded.*

*Values should not be mystical or complicated,
aspirational or manufactured. As shared by one of our
employees, they should be the foundation on which strategies
and plans are built. The foundation will always be there,
even though the plans and strategies may change."*

Sandra Looney Group HR Manager, Musgraves.

GREAT VIEW

Belief in not only the vision of the organisation but also in the values of the organisation is vital in order to motivate your people to move forward in the same direction.

The best companies 'partner' with all employees to get their input on the company values and how relevant those values are as the business moves on.

One organisation used to hold values workshops with all employees where they would explore the relevance of the company values on an ongoing basis. Just as the company has to be flexible in order to grow, the values may need to be reviewed in order to determine their relevance as the business grows. This exploration places the importance of values on everyone's agenda, it gets employees talking about them and it gets them to look at their own personal values and determine how relevant the values are to them and to the company. Creating a forum that places values on the agenda is a must-have for the modern organisation. Some companies bring in actors and get them to act out a scene that could happen in the workplace. Employees are then asked to consider the values in relation to the particular scene.

Cathal Divilly www.greatplacetowork.ie

The framed 'Mission Statement' that hangs proudly in many company reception areas doesn't necessarily prove employee connection. In the past, these statements were crafted by a scriptwriter or corporate board, reflected the views of a select few members of management, had little or nothing to do with values and were meaningless to most employees.

Indeed, if you put down a sample of mission statements on the table taken from different organisations, it would be likely that you could substitute one for the other and make no material difference to the company culture!

Today's organisations need to be fully inclusive and if a Mission Statement is to mean anything, it must reflect and be relevant to the employee's and the company's core values. At a micro level, the mission of the company must make the employee feel that their job is important

Not surprisingly a recent Gallup survey of more than 55,000 workers confirms that there were several attitudes that correlated strongly with higher profits. One of those attitudes was that the individuals made a direct connection between their work and the company's mission.

No connection = no future!

In January 2008, Howard Schultz, CEO of Starbucks, gathered his 4000 HQ staff and told them; "We need everyone in this room to believe in the mission of the company and if they don't, there's nothing wrong but you shouldn't be here!"

Give and Get Back

Increasingly the modern employee is motivated more by meaning over money.

Meaning and significance rank high on their hierarchy of values.

An Australian study found that 72% of Generation Y respondents will not apply for a position if they do not believe in what the organisation stands for. Source: http://hays.com.au/news

In 2004, 93% of UK teenagers agreed that "doing something you enjoy is more important than making a lot of money." England's future workforce believes that success is about happiness, not money, according to a report by the Learning and Skills Council (LSC).

The Irish Small Firms Association reported that exit interviews carried out during 2007 show that over 292,000 people left jobs for reasons other than money.

Companies are now responding by facilitating the search for meaning in peoples' lives. Corporate Social Responsibility is a growing focus for many progressive companies.

Every employee of Timberland, the giant US clothing company, is provided with up to 40 hours paid leave each year for community service.

Timberland's Path of Service™ program galvanizes the spirit of volunteerism and citizenship that permeates the company and seeks to engage the skills and talents of employees to create long-term solutions for critical community needs.

Today's employees want to know they're making a contribution to the organisation and to the world. They want to be involved and they want to feel valued. And their giving is translating into higher personal levels of happiness, which translates into higher productivity, which is good news for all. Meaning: win win

In research, funded by the Economic and Social Research Council, Professor Paul Whiteley and his team from Essex University identified a strong link between voluntary activity and life satisfaction.

Research involved sending questionnaires to 9,000 people and interviewed more than 3,000 people in detail about their lives.

"It seems that when we focus on the needs of others, we may also reap benefits ourselves. There is some psychological evidence that if people take part in volunteer activity, they feel better so it works at an individual level," said Professor Whiteley.

Exceed Their Expectations

In January 2008, for the second year running Google was voted Number 1 on Fortune 500's Best 100 Companies to Work for list.

To lure and keep workers, Google offers perks, including free cafeteria meals, free use of laundry machines, a child care centre, a free annual one-night ski trip, dog-friendly offices and an on-site doctor. Engineers can make a request to devote 20 percent of their time to projects of their choice. The Global Education Leave Program at Google allows employees to take a leave of absence for up to five years to pursue further education. On the Google ideas website, employees can give their thoughts on product or process improvements.

Many companies are now raising their game to keep employees engaged and happy. Flexible working days, paid paternity leave, 2 days paid leave for those getting married, August off but unpaid, compressed working weeks and many other initiatives are making many companies attractive places to work. Such initiatives are likely to precipitate positive word of mouth and convert employees into ambassadors for the company.

According to new research conducted by Cranfield School of Management in co-operation with the British Charity Working Families, there is a positive relationship between flexible working practices and employee performance. The report, 'Flexible Working and Performance', demonstrates that flexible working can be a win-win option for employers and employees.

Cultivate Community

The relationships people form with each other in the workplace are crucial to your employee's levels of job satisfaction and, by extension, their levels of productivity and, ultimately, your bottom line!

It's basic human nature to congregate. Put any group of strangers into a room and before too long they will naturally organise themselves into 'communities'. Being aware of this trait is very important so that you can maximise its benefits and minimise any potential negative impact!

Research, conducted by a team at Harvard University and Massachusetts General Hospital, found that productivity is largely affected by the quality of human relationships including cooperative, social group moods and interaction.

"I" to "We."

Gallup research has shown that employees who have best friends at work are seven times more likely to be engaged in their job.

More recent research by HR consultants Chiumento among 1000 adults found that three out of four said good relationships with workmates was the main reason they enjoyed their job. Fewer than half of those questioned cited financial rewards. Interestingly, the unhappier someone was at work, the more likely it was that they blamed the level of their salary.

In every community there will be leaders and followers, who are content with and have the potential to excel in their roles.

Try this exercise with a group of people: ask a challenging question e.g. how much of your brain potential do you tap into in a lifetime?

Watch the following pattern emerge as people answer. Normally the second and third answers will be plus or minus 15% of the first. This is particularly accurate if the first person is the leader in the subgroup. Oftentimes the first answer tends to be 50% in the majority of circumstances – right in the middle, a safe bet!

In the main very few people – i.e. a minority - will be deviant and not follow the pattern.

Applauding at an event is another example. You may have enjoyed the performance, but are you happy to be the first one to clap?

Cultivating this culture of community and reciprocation in your organisation will help you to create a great workplace, where people feel valued and involved.

And beware, friendships isn't a woolly concept. Don't think that your organisation will become a cosy talk shop; friendships equate to raw productivity.

GREAT VIEW

Fear of fun?

The area of 'fun in the workplace' is something that often frightens senior management. What does 'fun' mean? Does it mean the organisation will be like a holiday camp?

A sense of camaraderie is vital in every organisation. Camaraderie must be in place or developed in order for the maximum benefits of teamwork to be experienced by all.

The creation of forums that can act as a catalyst to develop camaraderie is an important task here. Ownership of these forums should be given to employees and they should cater for the entire organisation. So a social club is not about having a golf society anymore but about having clubs and forums to cater for all needs. Inclusivity, not isolation, is key.

Cathal Divilly www.greatplacetowork.ie

So in essence community is your cash cow. Fostering a sense of community in the workplace is critical.

Recruit Right!

The recruitment strategy should focus on attracting those with the right attitude, not just current ability. An applicant with a positive attitude and happy disposition may just be the right recruit.

A review of 225 relevant studies in Psychological Bulletin, published by the American Psychological Association, found that it's actually happiness that makes you succeed and not the other way around.

The review found that happy people are more likely to attempt new challenges and to push themselves to strive for fresh goals. They are also more likely to be liked by their peers, and thus recruited to better jobs and promoted to higher positions.

"Our review provides strong support that happiness, in many cases, leads to successful outcomes, rather than merely following from them," said one of the report's authors.

"Happy individuals are more likely than their less happy peers to have fulfilling marriages and relationships, high incomes, superior work performance, community involvement, robust health and even a long life."

Furthermore, brain researchers have found that activity in your prefrontal cortices — located behind your forehead - signifies idea generation and lively thought. Sadness decreases prefrontal cortical activity, while happiness increases it. If you tease that out, it means that happy people are more likely to have good ideas and think quickly, which often leads to success, and thus to increased wealth.

More proof of the positive effect of happiness comes from research from the University of Michigan in 2005: experiencing positive emotions on an ongoing basis helps you see the big picture.

"Negative emotions create a tunnel vision," said U-M psychology researcher Kareem Johnson. "Negative emotions like fear or anger are useful for short-term survival when there's an immediate danger like being chased by a dangerous animal. Positive emotions like joy and happiness are for long-term survival and promote big picture thinking, make you more inclusive and notice more details, make you think in terms of 'us' instead of 'them.'"

Furthermore, a person with the right attitude has the critical ability to attract teachers, circumstances and events to help them achieve any goals. They are also more authentic – the essential currency in the new business world.

Give me someone who would love to work with the company and has the right attitude – I will recruit on the spot regardless of current ability.

Many top companies understand this:

"We hire for attitude. We want people who like other people and are therefore motivated to serve them. Competence we can teach. Attitude is engrained." Isadore Sharp, Founder and CEO of the Four Seasons group speaking at the 2006 Great Place to Work Conference.

Low cost carrier, South West Airlines' philosophy is, 'We hire for attitude. We train for skill.'

I was involved in the interview process for the head of a technical department and my role was to assess each candidate's personality.

On paper, one individual seemed more than qualified for the position, however, as the interview proceeded, a very disturbing pattern emerged. He was very articulate and answered all the questions with relative ease but every time the MD spoke, this candidate appeared to switch off. Initially we thought that he was a little tired as the interview was after hours but in the second interview, the same pattern occurred. We speculated that he would not be much of a team player which he needed to be to excel in this organisation.

His attitude lost him the job.

In contrast many years ago I recruited a person for the post of trainer/admin manager even though, in theory, she wasn't qualified for the role. She had scraped through her final exams and her expertise was in typesetting, but in the interview she had proven to me that she was a very good listener and was willing to learn. She turned out to be a great trainer.

The world-famous Ritz Carlton hotel group are acutely aware of this crucial success strategy.

'At The Ritz-Carlton, our staff is the most important resource in our service commitment to our guests. Our motto states that "We are Ladies and Gentlemen serving Ladies and Gentlemen," and in doing so we create exceptional memories for our guests and for each other. Warmth and genuine caring are the hallmarks of every Ritz-Carlton employee. Every employee's contribution is valued and they are encouraged to fulfil individual aspirations. We trust each employee to use their creativity and accommodating personality to build strong relationships and provide a memorable experience to each guest.

Each employee is empowered. For example, when a guest has a problem or needs something special you should break away from your regular duties, address and resolve the issue."

GREAT VIEW

Companies seem to be quite good at making new employees feel welcome. The difficulty is ensuring that the person is the correct employee for the company in the first place. No matter what the latest buzzword is for recruitment – hire for fit etc - it is extremely difficult to ensure that the person you hire is the right person for the job. Anyone at an interview has their game face on (only natural) and because of that it's very difficult to get a true impression of how that person will actually fit in with the company.

As part of the interview process, some companies invite potential new employees on a social night out with the rest of the team to test potential camaraderie levels between any new and existing employees.

Cathal Divilly www.greatplacetowork.ie

As an aside, I have been having this interesting discussion with my colleagues in the entrepreneur development niche for years. I have advocated supporting the person regardless of the project on the premise that sooner or later the right attitude will attract the right project.

The ongoing goal must be to secure the best talent available in the marketplace and, even more importantly, to be seen as the company that develops and cultivates it. This reputation may help to give you the prestigious first pick in the marketplace.

Remember your potential employee is buying into an experience, not just a job. The person is accepting an opportunity to do something meaningful in their life, become part of a community that is making a difference, have fun and develop friendships within the organisation and be empowered by an inspired manager/leader.

Warning!

As you know from the first section, people tend to be attracted to people like themselves – the 'safe' option. Unfortunately this may mean that they say 'no' to the talented, energetic, candidate who challenges them and 'yes' to someone just like them who may not be what the company needs.

So, while seeking out energies that match our own is natural and healthy, every team needs a diverse range of skills, expertise and personalities to reach its full potential.

The right mix of like-minded, company-focussed individuals creates a powerful community.

Finally, not only do I believe that companies should recruit right; they should also show positive leadership in the context of how they let people go.

Redundancy can have a detrimental effect on people's confidence so interventions which help employees refocus and prepare mentally for the challenges ahead are very worthy practices e.g. Motivation, Communication, Rapport and Presentations training. Also the availability onsite of someone who can listen and empathise would be a distinct advantage. These activities are undertaken by many of the top companies.

In the long term, the company will benefit from positive P.R. and it will help reinforce the message that this is a great company to work for.

GREAT VIEW

In a market where employees can choose from a number of possible jobs to apply for it is essential that companies fighting for talent achieve Employer of Choice status. This is a vital message for companies to communicate to potential new candidates.

On average, the 50 Best Companies to Work for receive up to six times as many external job applications as there are number of employees.

Cathal Divilly www.greatplacetowork.ie

ASK!

More and more companies are asking visitors to pitch them their ideas. For many this represents the ultimate dream! Many successful websites and online businesses have been built on the vibrancy of their audience providing content. Think eBay, YouTube, Wikipedia and the hundreds of thousands of blogs and forums on every topic under the sun!

People create profits.

Probably one of the great examples of this was cited in the book Wikiconomics.

Goldcorp, a US mining company posted all its proprietary information on the internet and invited the public's interpretations (with cash incentives) of where the ore was located. The process brought the company from $100m in revenue to $9bn.

Transparency - trust not secrecy - is the way forward.

How can you ask?

Why not have your own RENTACROWD session to generate new ideas for your business? This involves inviting a small group from diverse backgrounds to brainstorm new ideas, potential improvements etc.

The rules of engagement are simple: every idea and opinion is noted and honoured regardless of how ridiculous it may seem.

This allows free flow and potential association.

Based on my own experience, I have found that the most creative ideas came from some weird and wonderful suggestions from my advisors.

Remember creativity happens where different ideas meet.

The Apple Genius Bar came from Steve Jobs' question 'how do we create a store that has the friendliness of a Four Seasons hotel?' The Four Seasons had been identified by a focus group as a place where you get the best service. The answer was 'put a bar in our shops, but not an alcohol bar - an advice bar!'

Business Week wrote this idea off before it even began and said 'Sorry Steve, Here's why Apple stores wont work' but Jobs persisted with his vision of "a buying experience as good as our products,' and in 2006 Apple had the highest annual sales per square foot ($4032) with Tiffany's trailing behind at $2,666

At a basic level, every company should host an internal forum/blog where employees can share and co-create new ideas for the business.

If your search is for new product ideas, why not incentivise it by giving employees a share of the revenue if their idea is implemented?

Model Off the Creative Mind

A study of genius by George Land and Beth Jarmin (published in 1993 in their book Breakpoint and Beyond) found that 98% of 2 - 5 year olds, 32% of all 8 – 10 year olds, 10% of all 13 – 15 year olds (in the group of 1,600 children tested) were in the creative genius category. Of the 200,000 adults surveyed, just 2% of those over 25 could be considered creative geniuses!

The challenge is to create a workplace where employees can revisit their natural state where creativity flourishes.

Now for a fascinating insight into an inventor's mind. Dr Louis Crowe is the inventor of such products as Slendertone Flex, Readpal, KneeHab and other medical products and is the author of upcoming title "Business, Sex and Innovation."

Genius At Work

"Innovation is just about making new connections that you or others may not have made or noticed before. Your mind is naturally wacky and creative. Just think of your dreams! This creative genius, within us all, is just suppressed when awake. You have to coax and tease the mind into revealing these ideas. If you make lots of crazy, wacky connections, maybe some of them might be useful or lead onto an even better idea.

Say you want to develop something new for coffee. You can use any cue to do this. It could even be the letter Q. This looks like a coffee cup from above except the handle isn't at

*a right angle to the cup. So could this be of benefit? It might
be easier to stack, pack, less likely to chip, etc. You'd have to
hold it at a different angle when drinking which could be
useful for people with some types of arthritis, etc. It may also
be easier to drink with your right hand? A mean left-handed
person could further modify the cup so that right-handed
people would stop stealing their mugs at work!*

*We often want to stir the coffee but the spoon is lost/
stolen/dirty so why not have an integrated spoon?*

*Or there is a snooker cue, a long pole. This could be used
in busy crowded coffee shops to transport the coffee cups back
to where they are needed. The cue is suspended at an angle
and the cups to be returned are just hooked on (handle is a
hook) and they slide down to where they are needed.*

*Or cue meaning a prompt or sign? For those drinking
tea you could print some tea leafs on the bottom. In the odd
cup, they may form a loose love heart or dollar sign.*

*Whilst these examples are deliberately mundane, they
illustrate that you can use anything to trigger an idea. So
if you want an idea in an area ... look around you and
make connections. See if there is any way you can make a
connection. You can think of people, places, theories, careers,
objects, etc. Don't worry if the connection makes little sense
or leads nowhere. You keep on making new connections and
sometimes something good will be triggered. Here are a few
pointers that I've found useful:*

Have lots of ideas. Don't try to have one world-beating

idea; have lots and maybe one will be good. The way to have one good idea is to have a hundred and throw out the 99 bad ones. A philosopher may say they are not bad as they led you to The One.

Look for a need, note what really irritates you. Whatever it is about a product or system that irritates you, can be improved upon. There is a better way, so find it!

Borrow ideas from related areas. If there is an innovation in tea shops, can you adopt it for your coffee shop?

Have fun. Play around with ideas. Discuss them with your friends. Try and make them laugh with some outlandish idea – that way there will be no pressure to suggest anything good. Have a competition for the stupidest idea.

Practice and question wherever you go. Whatever you see can be improved upon. How could you do it? It takes some practice, so persist.

Write them down, both the good and the bad. Not in long hand but just enough squiggles to jog your memory."

Daddy, I am ready!

Creativity isn't just the domain of people like Louis. Everybody has the seeds of creativity within.

> *"Every child is an artist. The problem is how to remain an artist once he grows up."*
>
> Pablo Picasso

Show Your Staff How to Switch Off

Convenience research done by my organisation conducted over the past two decades highlighted a few indisputable facts:

Stress affects everyone and has a negative effect on our productivity.

For the majority of my audiences stress equated to despair, as they had no clue how to reduce it's presence in their life.

When people started practising how to do nothing – five minutes a day for a month - they never looked back in terms of productivity and creativity.

Jon Kabat-Zinn and neuroscientist Richard Davidson, of the University of Wisconsin, found that after eight weeks of Mindfulness-Based Stress Reduction, a group of biotech employees showed a greater increase in activity in the left prefrontal cortex - the region of the brain associated with a happier state of mind - than colleagues who received no training. Remember happiness correlates to increased productivity.

The more you learn to still your mind, the more you feel connected directly with life, just like the child. And the more

Calm and Clarity!

connected you feel, the easier it is to see that path ahead, and make the right decisions.

Studying with the Quechuan Indians in 1996, I was to get my first lesson in doing nothing. I was challenged to find a place and sit in silence for two hours. High up in the Andes and surrounded by the most breathtaking scenery, I can remember sitting there questioning my idleness. My mind was buzzing with activity.

'When is something going to happen?' I wondered. 'I didn't come all the way across the world to learn nothing. I haven't the time. What's the point of doing nothing? What am I learning?' The quieter I became physically, the louder and louder my mind appeared to be. 'Is this nothingness the catalyst for insanity?' I thought.

I eventually recognised that this inner noise had been always there, and the only difference now was that I was listening. Once every thought was acknowledged, it allowed me to return my focus to the beautiful scenery. Another thought – acknowledge – refocus and so on. Gradually, the gap between my thoughts started to widen, and the noise began to subside, little by little.

Now whenever I feel stressed, lacking energy, experiencing writer's block or unclear in my decision-making; I go down to the sea and focus on the movement or the sound of the waves. As is normal, thoughts pop into my mind but, after acknowledging them, my focus returns to the waves.

"The ocean disentangles the netted mind."

Anonymous

Take Action!

Find a comfortable place to sit where you will not be disturbed. Switch off your phone! Sit with your back straight, shoulders relaxed and chin slightly tucked in. Ensure that your knees are lower than your hips, and allow your hands to rest on your thighs. Allow your eyes to close. Now, simply focus on your breath as it comes in and goes out. Just listen to yourself inhaling and exhaling.

Your conscious mind will immediately try to fill the silence with chatter but as each thought arrives simply say, 'Wel-come. Wel-go' and go back to listening to your breath. Don't try to ignore them or make them go away. Simply acknowledge them, and turn your attention back to focussing on your breathing.

At first, you will probably find yourself saying 'Wel-come. Wel-go' much more than you are listening to your breath, but with practice, the gaps between your thoughts become longer and longer.

If you do not like to sit still, you can achieve the same level of stillness while walking. Just focus on your breath, the sensation of your feet on the ground, the wind on your face or the sounds around you. Acknowledge any thoughts that arise and refocus.

Another alternative is to purchase a nature CD, focus on the music, acknowledge any stray thoughts and refocus and so on.

The more you practice relaxing and tapping into that inner space of stillness, the easier and more beneficial it gets. Watch your productivity, problem solving, clarity, creativity and indeed intuitive capacity improve – all by doing nothing!

Trust Wisdom Over Knowledge

"Don't let the noise of other people drown out your inner voice. And most importantly, have the courage to follow your heart and intuition. They somehow already know what you truly want to become."

Steve Jobs, CEO of Apple Computer
and Pixar Animation Studios.
(Presentation delivered at
Stanford University June 2006)

Long before the mobile phone market exploded, Nokia employed world-class designers to create multi-coloured, fashionable devices on a hunch that the demand would stretch far beyond the limited commercial usage that was being predicted by experts. As a result, Nokia is now one of the most instantly recognised and valuable brands in the world.

Information kills ideas

Story – Best-Selling Guidance

In 1996, my intuition was telling me to write a best-selling personal excellence book. To start the process, I printed "I am a Best Selling author" and "Manuscript finished by May 28th" and placed the A4 sheets on the back of my office door and over my workspace.

My friends and business colleagues highlighted the obvious obstacles that lay ahead:

English was not my strongest subject. In my final examination, I earned just a very poor 'D' grade.

Writing and speaking are two very different disciplines, and I had no experience of writing.

Famous American writers predominantly controlled the self-help market.

There was also a view that I was too young to be taken seriously, and we didn't even discuss how I was going to find a publisher or motivate people to buy my book!

It's fair to say that the prevailing 'wisdom' was against my adventure, but with trust in my heart, I swam against this considerable tide to honour my inner whispers.

> *You see things; and you say, "Why?" But I dream things that never were; and I say, "Why not?"*
>
> George Bernard Shaw

My focus remained on the dream, believing as always that the map would appear in time.

Over the next week and months, people turned up, doors opened and opportunities presented themselves until, by May 28th, the manuscript was finished!

To date "How? When You Don't Know How" has been a mega best seller. Mission accomplished.

It is important to note that right throughout the process I continued to focus on my dream and worked continuously to convert it into reality. This meant that no matter what town I visited, I called to bookshops to merchandise and sign books. Furthermore, I initiated publicity in all my target regions, and never missed an opportunity to tell people about the book.

Commitment counts!

Your logical, left-brain mind will always give you enough reasons not to act on your gut feelings. No matter what your dream is, you will always find enough reasons not to act.

Whether or not you are aware of it, you have access to an intelligence far greater than that which is available through your conscious mind: your intuition.

Trusting and following your intuition, gut feeling, sixth sense, hunch - or whatever you want to call it – is an integral part of reaching your full potential, personally and professionally. In my own life, my intuition is my compass.

Story - The Breath of Possibility
Pat McKeown, AsthmaCare

I had asthma from a very young age. I was often caught for breath and had to stay in bed because I did not have enough air to physically move. By the time I was in my early twenties I was on high doses of medication to control the asthma.

In 1997, I graduated from Trinity College Dublin and started work.

I stumbled across an article about a Russian doctor, Konstantin Buteyko, who claimed to know how to reverse the cause of asthma. Upon further enquiry, I contacted people in Australia and learned more about the technique. Logically it made sound sense - breathe through your nose and keep your breathing quiet. Simple as it seems, Buteyko discovered that the cause of asthma is over breathing. By using his methods, my asthma improved dramatically!

When I was a full two years symptom and medication free and still in the same job, I realised that I wasn't happy. Something was missing from my life and an emptiness or hollowness prevailed. Driving to my hometown, the thought struck me that asthmatics should be made aware of correct breathing and other lifestyle factors. There was no doubt that it worked. I was living proof!

That weekend was a momentous one for me. It felt as though a weight had been lifted from me and even though I had not thought about the intricacies of starting a business, I had an overwhelming comfort that everything was going to be all right. I contacted the Buteyko clinic of Moscow and by 2002 had completed my training.

As I think back, I can see that if I had given starting a business much thought AsthmaCare would not exist! I was entering an area that was traditionally the domain of doctors and the pharmaceutical industry. I was also aware that some people around me thought I was mad. However, the overwhelming feeling that I experienced that weekend - that I was not going to fail - became the driving force behind my work.

I am now one of a few people who can say that they love their job. I apply myself to it effortlessly. In the past six years, I have written several books including the best seller Asthma Free Naturally. Thousands of asthma patients have attended my clinics and AsthmaCare is now taught in seven countries. There is no stress in this, nor is there much effort. www.asthmacare.ie

Your challenge now is to identify how your intuition delivers for you. Does it manifest as an inner voice, a vision or a feeling?

Become aware of the messages your gut is sending you. Watch out for those apparent coincidences, those 'chance meetings', that inner wisdom or gut feeling.

Do you remember the last time you met someone and you had this feeling about them, positive or negative - maybe you decided to disregard this wisdom to your cost?

We receive intuitive messages all the time - from the radio, from idle conversations or from our 'sixth sense'. Simply tune in for your answers. Awareness is paramount.

Use your intuition regularly now and it will become a powerful force in your life. More amazingly, it will attract into your life circumstances, people and information that will help you achieve your goal and I can guarantee that you will end up in a place you recognise as better than your starting point.

> *"Most of entrepreneurship, for me, is about instinct and intuition. Many times I have been asked by someone considering a new venture if he/she should go for it. But an entrepreneur knows instinctively when to go for it."*
>
> Michael Dell, Founder of Dell

Value Feedback Over Failure

According to Global Entrepreneurial Monitor (GEM) fear of failure is the top reason given worldwide by aspiring entrepreneurs for not starting their own businesses.

NESTA - the National Endowment for Science, Technology and the Arts and the UK's largest early stage investor in innovative and creative businesses – found that almost three quarters of people who said they had what they believed was a good business idea were not acting on it because they were afraid of not succeeding.

Ironically, all the research confirms that would-be entrepreneurs and potential leaders all over the world are being strangled by something that doesn't exist.

That's right! Failure is a myth!

Conventional wisdom would not agree with that statement. Wikipedia even states, 'Failure in general refers to the state or condition of not meeting a desirable or intended objective. It may be viewed as the opposite of success.'

However, the greatest entrepreneurs in history would be on my side!

Thomas Edison, inventor of the light bulb famously said, "I have not failed. I've just found 10,000 ways that won't work."

It took James Dyson, the engineer who reinvented the vacuum cleaner, four and a half years and 5,127 prototypes to refine his design.

"Each failure taught me so much," he said. "Success teaches you nothing. Failures teach you everything. Making mistakes is the most important thing you can do."

Failure = Feedback

"Invariably we try ten things that don't quite work out in order to do one thing that is successful. And we learn a lot in doing the ten things that didn't quite work." Larry Page, inventor of Google

Once, when a colleague made a mistake that cost Google several million dollars, Larry Page told her 'I'm so glad you made this mistake because I want to run a company where we are moving too quickly, and doing too much, not being too cautious and doing too little. If we don't have any of these mistakes, we're just not taking enough risk.'

Fortune Magazine's list of World's Most Admired Companies reveals some interesting facts about the attitude to failure in the context of innovation within the workplace.

The two companies that lead the field in this respect factor in failure as an inevitable and important part of the creative process and allow for 82% of innovative ideas to fail without penalties. The other companies in Fortune's Most Admired list allow 70% of innovative ideas to fail without penalties.

So, the world's greatest companies create a winning culture, where innovative thinking is actively encouraged and failure plays an important role.

Teresa Amabile Entrepreneurial Management Unit at Harvard Business School collected nearly 12,000 daily journal entries from 238 people working on creative projects in seven companies. Her findings confirmed that joy, not fear, is the best catalyst for idea generation and, as expected, collaboration beats competition.

Another finding was that creativity is not just the domain of creative types - everyone can be creative.

Programmed For Success

As a child, 'Never say die', 'Have no fear', 'Try and try again', 'Enjoy the moment', were your working metaphors. Choose now to revisit and reuse these winning thought processes. Look at the way a toddler attacks life with energy, enthusiasm and curiosity – and without fear!

By the age of two most people have learned to walk. It's a very interesting process. One day, something inside you tells you that you want to be able to do more than crawl around on the floor. So you pull yourself up on your feet, using whatever is around to help you. You're a bit shaky at first and you end up sitting on the floor a lot but you gradually get steadier on your feet and more confident. Before long, you can navigate the room using the furniture as a prop. Then it happens! You want to get from A to B but there is nothing to hold onto! You're going to have walk all by yourself!

You fix your eye on the goal – where you want to go – and you launch yourself from the security of the armchair into open space. You take a step – wobble a bit – steady yourself. Take another step. Then land on your backside!

What happens then? Do you give up? Do you say to yourself 'I tried my best and I can't do it.'? It hurts. I'm never doing that again!'? Did your ego kick in and start whispering 'you're making a fool of yourself. They're all laughing at you! Better quit while you are ahead'?

If that is as far as any of us were prepared to go, we would all be walking around holding onto solid objects for support!

By the age of five you had acquired a vocabulary of over eighty per cent of the words necessary to communicate daily. Imagine now attempting to become proficient in a new language, without the aid of any direct instruction, textbooks or tutorials. It seems like quite a challenge, but for the 'uninhibited child' - free from the chains of social conditioning - everything is possible. You didn't care that you got it wrong a lot of the time. You were not discouraged when people couldn't understand you or laughed at you. You just kept on doing your best until you mastered the language.

Children are fearless adventurers. In their world there is no such thing as failure – only feedback! They know instinctively that to discover what works best, you must first discover what doesn't work! Today, do you accept that every failure is bringing you closer to your dreams?

You may argue that learning to walk and talk is instinctual, but I believe that the desire to reach our full potential is equally so.

We are all programmed for success, but we integrate limitations from our environment.

Both individually and collectively, the only failure in life is the failure to learn from failure.

Not allowing people to fail in your organisation is the same thing as celebrating middle-of-the-road performances from your staff.

In A Nutshell

Unleashing the Creative Potential of Employees Is the Key to Your Success

Give your employees quality attention by:

- Trusting them

- Keeping them informed

- Investing in them

- Engaging them in a meaningful way

- Giving them more than money

- Exceeding their expectations

- Cultivating community

- Recruiting right!

- Asking

- Modelling off the creative mind

- Showing your staff how to switch off

- Trusting wisdom over knowledge

- Valuing feedback over failure

Section 3

Get Personal

"Literary education is of no value, if it is not able to build up a sound character."

Gandhi

In any business or organisation, getting the best from your employees and customers is essential.

The first section outlined the strategies for dealing with your customers in these challenging times.

The second section illustrated how you can recognise and leverage the full potential of your employees.

Now that you've got an insight into the people who will be crucial to your business, from now on, and explored how to make the most of every opportunity, it's time to look in the mirror!

Character not celebrity

According to Stanford Business School Advisory Board, self-awareness has been recognised as the most important capability for leaders to develop.

It doesn't matter how well you understand your organisation or how well you understand you employees and customers, until you have a deep understanding of yourself – what makes you tick, what motivates and inspires you – you are missing a critical piece of the puzzle.

In the context of taking the trip towards self-awareness - a place where you will recognise that you have all the resources required to unleash your potential, indeed a place where being authentic is the only reality - the first step is to understand your starting point.

Very simply: you should appreciate that not only are you the problem, you are also the solution.

Moreover it is possible that your greatest obstacle is you!

Your mindset may be your greatest challenge.

People do as you do, not as you say, so whoever you are, whatever you do will be mirrored in your staff's activities. Employees need to know you care. When you are authentic, you project this effortlessly.

Research has shown that, for most employees, the most important person in an organisation is their direct line manager and not the CEO.

The relationship built between managers and their line will have a major impact on your bottom line.

Luck or Design?

"Why bother? Sure, it is all luck." We've all heard it said about successful people in every field. In other words, those that make money or are successful are lucky, not strategic. Is it possible to ride on the coat tails of luck all your life or is there a strategy which when adopted can open the doors?

I believe the latter.

Interestingly, a study was conducted with millionaires and non-millionaires on the BBC series "Mind of the Millionaire." The objective of the study was to highlight the two group's opinions toward the effect of luck in the process. The first group (the millionaires) believed that luck wasn't the reason for their success. The second group (the non-millionaires) came back with a resounding "yes!" it is all luck!

So it isn't luck and there is even more!

Based on years and years pushing entrepreneurs through their doors Professor Ken Morse from the MIT Entrepreneurship Centre in Boston shares my 100% conviction that entrepreneurs are not just born, they are made.

How can you develop the mindset and attributes of the new manager/entrepreneur /leader?

An inside out approach is required!

Take A Conscious Trip

Yes, your greatest obstacle is you!

More specifically, the years of programming lodged in your subconscious (or other than conscious mind) could be holding you back. As you're about to find out, consciously you are limited but subconsciously you are unlimited.

First, here's a quick insight into the critical difference between your conscious and subconscious mind.

Take Action!

You need two pens for this exercise.

Draw a circle with your left hand and a circle with your right hand at the same time.

Pause

Now, something even easier –draw a circle with your right hand and a square with your left hand simultaneously.

It is ok to draw a square with your right hand and a circle with your left hand at the same time if you so wish!

How did you get on?

It is likely that the first task wasn't a challenge. Why?

Because I asked you to do one thing at any one time in your conscious mind i.e. draw a circle with both hands.

The second part is not so easy. Because now I am asking you to consciously do two things at the one time. This is a challenge too far for many. Indeed Leonardo da Vinci was one of the few that could do this. Now I know many women will claim they can multitask, but they can't do it consciously – only subconsciously!

Doing two things at any one time in your conscious mind for most is impossible.

However it is possible to execute many tasks simultaneously in your subconscious. For example, the majority of people will admit that random thoughts pop in and out of their mind no matter how engaging the material is. So you could say that your thoughts are been produced by your 'other than conscious' mind as you sit there.

You also know that new cells are been produced all the time so it is fair to say that each person is continuously recreating their body, again outside conscious control

Also of course you are breathing – again outside conscious control.

You don't have to stop mid sentence and say to yourself, "I will have another five hundred breaths please!"

Was there ever an occasion in the past where while driving long distance, you could not recall driving through some town or village on the way. You have been on autopilot – isn't that scary?

It appears that we also have let's call it a protection mechanism in our subconscious or other than conscious facility.

Also and most importantly logged in our subconscious are our attitudes and beliefs about life – our life's metaphors, all the positive and negative ones.

As there is an intimate link between our psychology the way we think, which is logged in our subconscious, and our physiology – the way we look, posture, voice projection etc, a persons attitudes and beliefs will be easy to detect – all you have to do is to sharpen your senses.

A few other interesting things to consider about your subconscious:

It acts like a computer so garbage in, garbage out. Some calculate that about 60,000 thoughts zip through your mind on a daily basis – ninety per cent of those the same as the previous day. Thus if you continue with the same thought process, you can expect the same results.

One study suggested that for every positive message a day a person receives, they are exposed to eight negatives.

A few years ago I did a study with five hundred students - the ratio of negative to positive messages at a conscious level was two is to one. It does appear that the bias in the main is towards the negative.

So Where Is The Power? In The Subconscious!

The next step requires an understanding of what's lodged in your subconscious. Identification is the first step towards unleashing your potential.

Your subconscious truths, not your conscious spin, are what we are seeking.

Take Action!

Record your immediate response to this question:
A man and his son are involved in a very serious car accident. The man dies at the scene. The son is rushed into casualty. The doctor on duty on seeing the boy shouts out "this is my son". Who is the doctor?

I have given this exercise to thousands of people worldwide and about half of them know the right answer straight away, and the others are completely perplexed.

Interestingly I was part of the second group, as was a female medical consultant and a male doctor friend.

The answer is; the doctor was the child's mother!

What stops us from correctly answering a simple question like that?

In my case, my subconscious had obviously associated the word 'Doctor' with males and so strong was this association that the thought that the doctor could be female simply didn't register. An even more important deduction from this exercise is that if you had asked me beforehand, I would have consciously said that of course there are male and female doctors, because these are my conscious truths. But the fact is that my true reality – what was logged in my subconscious – was that there are only male doctors, which is why I could not answer the question correctly.

Now consider the possibility that you have many associations positive and negative about entrepreneurship, motivating people, leadership and reaching your own potential that may be stopping you from moving to the next level.

So how do you discover your personal truths? Look at your results in life for a true insight into your thinking.

For example:

Have you tapped into your true potential or has life been one hard struggle?

Are you at least doing something practical about developing your business idea or are you still 'all talk'?

What is your biology saying about your autobiography? Do you look happy and healthy or tired and stressed? If people cannot see that you love what you do, something's up! You are in the wrong place.

Are you attracting positive, helpful people who will contribute to moving you closer to your goal or prophets of doom who drag you down?

How is your language? Do you find yourself using self-deprecating words like 'should', can't' 'might' 'but' 'never' 'problem' or uplifting words like 'will' 'can' 'always' 'challenge'? (Note: Go to www.kevinkellyunlimited.com/personalaudit and take the Personal Audit™ now for an in-depth insight into who you are, what makes you tick, what's driving you and what is holding you back.)

Now consider your current processes. Are you paying lip service to your people or have you created structures that allows employees the opportunity for training and development, a forum to express their opinions, and constructive evaluation of their performance, an opportunity to share their ideas and so on?

> *"The actions of men are the best interpreters of their thoughts."*
>
> James Joyce

Learn From Others

"Why restrict yourself to the narrow "I" when the whole world is yours." Hindu Wisdom

Identify your limiting beliefs and patterns is usually the difficult part; solving them is often easier.

Probably one of the greatest challenges is ego – the illusionary I - or the story you have told yourself about yourself.

Answer the following questions honestly to clarify whether or not your ego is hampering your potential.

Are you fearful of saying "I don't know" when this is the appropriate response?

Are you always on the lookout for opportunities to create leaders at every level in your organization?

Are you willing to move outside your comfort zone?

Do you recruit the best talent for each job or those you believe you can control?

"Make a fool of yourself. Otherwise you won't survive."
Richard Branson

As a leader, entrepreneur or businessperson have you pinpointed potential mentors and teachers who have walked the path before you? Are you open to learning from everybody you meet, regardless of age, education, wealth, race or gender? Do you believe that the teacher can become the student and vice versa?

Do you spend a lot of time defending your point of view?

Warning!

There is no such thing as reality, only your interpretation of it so be open to the fact that your version may not be the best one!

Fifteen years ago, I truly believed that success and happiness were dependent on and measured by money and material possessions – and I was right. When I spoke about life strategy to audiences around the world, I was completely right in what I was saying, based on my beliefs at that time.

Today, with a totally different understanding of, and insight into, what constitutes success and happiness, I am right also. I now recognise that back then I was only right in my own mind.

This understanding has given me a more open, maybe more humble, view of my convictions today. My mind is now always open to new teachers, because even the most unlikely person I meet could have something to teach me.

For example we all recognise that children can be wonderful teachers but how many of us dare to integrate the simple wisdom we can learn from a child's view of the world into our lives?

A few years back a former student of mine called wondering if I could help her brother who was penning his first publication in the IT segment. A few days later we met. At the end of the meeting he asked me how he could help as a "thank you" for my time and ideas. He was a website designer and was happy to return the favour. He persisted in his request and I finally conceded. I discovered that he had worked on very high profile online projects including work with Warner music, one of the first online magazines and online banks.

At zero cost to me, this man designed a website that has consistently maintained a number one search engine ranking in many key phrases. The student had become the teacher. This is just one of many similar experiences in my lifetime.

Entrepreneurs tend to specialise in one specific area of their business. Integrating the philosophy that there are teachers everywhere allows them to attract complementary skills, create a winning team and geometrically increase the possibility that their venture will be a success.

There are zero degrees of separation from potential teachers, circumstances and events if you have the right mindset.

There are leaders, guides and mentors everywhere, at every level in your organisation. You only have to look around you and be willing to see beyond the labels!

Approaching potential teachers with a win-win mentality will help bring your career to the next level.

Sixteen thousand feet up in the Andes in Peru, when two Q'uero Indians meet for the first time, often they set a challenge. Let's say the challenge is a race. Whoever wins the race is duty bound to coach the loser until he has attained a similar competency. In return the loser teaches the victor a new skill. This interdependence helps both people. Both win, as does their society. Indeed, everybody is the same in their eyes. As they say, 'We are all just energy.' Ayni, the art of reciprocation, ensures that their society as a whole grows together.

Finally select your advisors wisely.

If you're going to climb a mountain and you need a guide, you should look for somebody with personal experience and local knowledge rather than a person who dreams, talks, writes, paints or sings about climbing the mountain!

The same analogy can be applied to any challenge you face. In life and in business, a mentor with personal experience and local knowledge is much more valuable than one who is all talk.

So select your advisors wisely!

Seek out the Sherpa as opposed to the superstar!

Choose Differently

We all have many well-established thought patterns wired into our nervous systems to enable us to act without thinking. Some are vital for our survival and others limit our potential.

A pattern works very like a muscle – the more you use it, the stronger it gets. The more attention you give to a thought or the more you repeat a pattern, the stronger the connections become in your nervous system.

To disempower limiting patterns, you need to fully integrate one powerful statement into your being:

Choose Differently!

I suggest you write down these two words now and review regularly.

The next time you find yourself faced with any challenge, stop yourself reacting without thinking and repeating a familiar pattern.

For example many people have been engrained with the belief that 'Security is good'. This was the reality for one course participant in the past. This belief meant that she always sought out the safe option in any situation and could never make a bold decision. She was stuck in a rut because her inner voice was telling her 'security is good' and preventing her from moving forward.

As soon as she identified this limiting belief and realised that the opposite of security is fearlessness, she was able to make more empowering choices when faced with any challenge.

Unfortunately some choose to continue to honour a disempowering belief to their detriment. I know a would-be entrepreneur who sat on two brilliant ideas that are now worldwide success stories for somebody else – because he failed to face and floor his fears and to take action.

The key is to do the opposite of what your fear is telling you to do! Someday, I'm going to do a bungee jump. The real challenge is that I am afraid of heights! To overcome this fear and prepare myself for my bungee jump, I make a point of going across the high ropes at every opportunity at our local adventure centre. It doesn't matter that I am afraid, or that there are large pools of sweat underneath the ropes! All that matters is that I am feeling the fear – and doing it anyway. The sense of exhilaration and achievement when I get back to earth again is indescribable and worth every drop of sweat! Over time, I know that I will condition myself to reduce my fear of heights until I can make that jump over the precipice.

Become aware of your thoughts so that you can find, feel and floor your fears once and for all. With practice, practice and more practice, pushing yourself a little further each time, you can replace any limiting belief or pattern with a more empowering choice, but it all starts with the decision to choose differently.

Focus Over Fear

Another way of disempowering limiting beliefs and tapping into your potential is pursuing a goal that is congruent with your values. When you focus on any goal, you have a natural ability to attract the support and information necessary for success.

The fact is that you have already used this strategy - maybe outside your conscious attention with great effect while making some important material decisions, for example while moving house or buying a car or locating a business premises. Because of their relative importance, we invest a significant amount of time and energy on them. When you think about anything at length it moves from your conscious to your subconscious mind. This is a verifiable scientific fact. You actually create new neural pathways in your brain! The more you think about something, the stronger the connections become in your nervous system and the more deeply ingrained it becomes. Your subconscious has an efficient filtering system that, on instruction, will help you see what you want to see and attract what you need to attract.

For instance, as soon as you decided to change your car, have you noticed how new car dealerships seem to suddenly appear out of nowhere?

When you read the daily papers, it appears like there was nothing but car adverts on every page!

As for the TV and radio, it seemed as if the motor industry is their only source of advertising revenue!

After you bought the car you began to see the exact same make, model and colour everywhere!

As mentioned earlier, we are all hardwired for success. The programming is in place. You just need to re-activate it!

This strategy can be used for all your goals and dreams from attempts to develop your domestic market to in my case developing an international presence. However your goals must be underpinned by positive intent.

Compare Yourself to Yourself

To succeed, your focus should be 100% on your own performance.

A 2003 study of 16,266 people at 886 companies in the UK found rank had a bigger effect on happiness than pay level.

More recent research from Firebaugh and Tach found many people's happiness level are determined on how well they are doing relative to their peers.

A few years ago, I started conducting a survey with course attendants. The following propositions were put on the table:

Option one: I offered them a salary of €50,000 and everyone they knew would earn €25,000.

Option two was an offer of a salary of €100,000 with everyone they knew earning €250,000.

The attendees were then told that all other factors were equal. Naively I thought it was a simple choice – €50k or €100k – but this wasn't the case! To my amazement, a significant minority choose the first option and many (and I mean many) had to think about their answer.

Obviously companies must be cognisant of this fact if they want to build a positive empowered community. By the way, comparing yourself to others is the direct route to a lifetime of stress and missed opportunities.

Compare yourself to your best self if you want to tap into your potential.

Mission Possible

In organisations and as individuals, the ideal is to ensure that we are living and following our mission. Our goals and activities should not bring us in an opposite direction, otherwise we have disconnected!

When an organisation focuses on a mission that reflects the dreams and values of all employees, it creates a culture in which creativity and loyalty flourish.

At a personal level, the dream is to turn your passion into profit, to make a living from following your bliss, and this is more than possible.

People who do what they love are invariably one of the best in their field for which they will be rewarded.

Moreover as shown in my own life, I believe that when mission, contribution and conscience collide, provision is the by-product. Each time on my own personal journey when a financial crisis loomed large, something turned up.

Story – Wrong Flight, Right Seat

In 1998, eight years after starting a business consultancy and twelve months after publishing my first book, my trusted intuition, was promoting a most challenging plan i.e. to turn my back on my lucrative career as a successful, very well-paid Marketing Consultant, say goodbye to my six figure turnover and follow my new found bliss – motivation/personal development training with a focus on making a real difference in people's lives.

Intuitive promptings, hunches, inner whispers, divine guidance, call it what you like, certainly didn't come complete with pension plan!

Within months, I went from high income to less than the average industrial wage.

In an effort to repay my crippling debt, I re-mortgaged my house and left for the USA. After three very challenging months, I came back to Ireland for a short break.

Getting a return flight to San Francisco was more difficult than I thought it would be. Monday was my preferred day to travel. No joy. Okay, Tuesday would do. No joy. At a pinch, Wednesday would suffice. Nothing doing. Finally I got a flight out Thursday. On the Dublin to London leg of the flight, I sat beside a very pleasant woman who engaged me in conversation. In economy note! She was head of the training department of one of Fortune 500's top ten companies. Half way through the conversation, she committed herself to opening up the US market for me. A case of being on the right seat on the right plane at the right time!

A week later, honouring her commitment, she booked me for a very important engagement with her trainers. Considering the situation, this was a "blow away" bonus in every sense of the word. This appointment would open up the whole market for my training package if it was successful. In this business as in most, the first question decision-makers posed was "Who have you worked for in the past?" I hadn't much of an answer and needed 'the start' as they say in Ireland. Afraid of making any mistakes, the week before the event, I asked my contact for an idea of an appropriate price to charge. My poker face almost slipped at the figure she mentioned. This was going to be the most lucrative assignment in my career to date. I was blown away. To put it in context, my "lucky seat" had just delivered close to the equivalent of a year's turnover! A lot less would have done me!

Living your mission is the ultimate authentic life and guarantees a life of magic and adventure!

> *"Yes, I am a dreamer. For a dreamer is one who can find his way by moonlight and see the dawn before the rest of the world."*
> Oscar Wilde

Time to Act

So finally we come to what for many people is the longest bridge to cross – the one that brings you from inaction to action.

Consider the following:

If your life span is 80 years from birth to death, you have approximately 2,522,880,000 seconds to live. Since you started reading this paragraph, you have used up about 20 of them. If you go back and check how long it took you to read the paragraph you will use up another 20. Tonight, you will spend 86,400 of your precious seconds asleep. In fact, assuming you sleep 8 hours a night, you will be unconscious for 1/3 of your life. The clock is ticking. When you reach the end of your time, death is waiting for you. That is a certainty. Which do you fear most, living or dying?

Tick, tick, tick….

Take action now!

When you truly start living, watch the positive effect it has on your life, your team and your organisation.

In A Nutshell

It's All About You!

Find your personal power by:

- Taking a conscious trip

- Tuning into the subconscious!

- Learning from others

- Choosing differently

- Developing focus over fear

- Comparing yourself to yourself

- Living your mission

- Taking action now

Biography

Kevin Kelly is an Internationally Acclaimed Motivational Speaker and authority on entrepreneurship, leadership, sales, creativity and personal excellence.

After graduating with a Commerce degree in 1987, he proceeded to break sales record in each of the companies his worked for.

Over the past two decades, he has keynoted at events around the world including the Middle East, Far East, Europe and the US.

Whether it is a one-hour keynote speech or a one-day seminar, Kevin has the ability to engage people one hundred per cent in his interactive experiences. His results speak for themselves - four presentations in Monaco, Edinburgh, Colorado and Tehran recorded a 4.5 out of five average. Kevin weaves his magic with a cocktail of exercises, information and stories that are based on his unique experiences around the world, inside and outside corporate corridors. From challenging himself to write a Best Seller even though limited by a poor grade in English, to going from high income to low income and back when he decided to follow his passion, to breaking sales records in many companies, Kevin more than walks the path of his own philosophies.

Born in the West of Ireland where he still lives with his wife Deirdre and son Conor, his other book titles include his Business Book "Basics before Buzz" and "Life: A Trip Towards Trust." In addition, he has produced three motivational CD's Good Enough - Now go get it; Setting, getting and forgetting Goals and Compelling Communication Strategies. (All now translated into Farci.)

Kevin has appeared many times on National TV and radio shows in Ireland, UK, USA and most recently featured on the front page of Success Magazine in Iran.

"Honesty, Integrity and Passion" - these are the three things you get when you recruit Kevin as a Motivational Keynote speaker according to research conducted amongst his key customers.

If you want a ROI (return on investment) from your next keynote speaker choose Kevin - authentic, engaging and results driven.

What Others Say About Kevin

"We engaged Kevin to speak to our entire workforce a number of months prior to the business closing. We were looking for an alternative means to invigorate people and to instil a positive outlook in an inherently negative situation. Kevin Kelly delivered. His sessions focused on job searching, self-marketing and self-belief. Feedback was universally positive and an exercise we were delighted to have delivered to our folks."

John O'Donovan, Director of Operations.
Boston Scientific Tullamore

"Some speakers motivate and some have great content. Kevin Kelly has both which means he brings double the value to your conference. If you want a speaker who will inspire, motivate, educate, entertain and give a performance so powerful that the delegates will hardly dare blink for missing something then Kelly is your man."

David Thomas, World Memory Champion,
International speaker, and
Sunday Times #1 Best Selling Author,
www.TheMotivationSpeaker.com

""Kevin is motivational, inspiring and enthusiastic, not to mention lively, entertaining and thought-provoking. His energy was transferred onto his audience as he engaged with them throughout. He encouraged self-belief and instilled the importance of positive thinking. He certainly offered something different!"

Cathal Divilly, Managing Director,
Great Place to Work® Institute Ireland
www.greatplacetowork.ie

"I really enjoyed your interactive and inspirational keynote at the PMI Leadership meeting in Budapest. Your energy and content was inspiring."

Thangavel Subbu, PMI ISSIG

"The feedback to Kevin Kelly was very positive - most people in addition to have been entertained and informed, took some vignette or tool away from the talk that should have a positive impact on their work performance in the future."

Karen Fitzsimons, Davis Langdon
Top 50 Best Companies to Work for 2008 www.dlpks.ie

"Too often speakers base their presentations on other people's experiences. Kevin has lived and breathed every bit of the journey he takes you on. That's what makes him stand out head and shoulders above every other speaker I have seen in the last 15 years. Yesterday Kevin's motivational keynote took 30 colleagues and me on a rollercoaster ride for three hours. Initially it was scary, then the adrenalin pumped through all our veins and when he eventually allowed us to loosen our grip we all walked away shattered but taking with us the experience of a lifetime.

The energy with which he delivers is breathtaking - it's akin to Michael Schumacher on steroids!" The seminar lasted three hours - the impact will be forever."

Michael Brady, CEO 98FM
"Radio Station of the Year 2008"

"Kevin Kelly is truly inspirational. He not only talks the talk but walks the walk and this has enhanced his creditability. Our staff, who have encountered him through our corporate programmes on Leadership and motivation, have given him a 100% approval rating. He has always adapted his presentation to suit our particular needs - truly flexible, always relevant and ever optimistic."

Harry McCarry,
Head of Staff Development, Belfast Institute

*"A mixture of energy, entertainment and high content.
Kevin's inspirational "timeless truths" were delivered with
clarity and in a style that honours his Irish upbringing."*
Ray O Flaherty , Chairman and Founder,
All-Ireland/U.S. Chamber of Commerce.

*"I have seen Kevin perform at three very different events and
I was struck by his effective communication. Unlike so many
people he communicates very well in his own unique and
passionate style. He has a message to tell and he wants his
audience to benefit. When he is not "on tour" his website is a
good place to visit for stimulation. A man with a vision!*
Michael McDonagh, Commercial Director,
Adesco Nutricines Limited

*"Staff from all levels of the company found the sessions with
Kevin to be a great experience and quite unique. They were
grateful for the chance to be involved in training which
focused on life as a whole, not just on work. Well done!"*
David J. Steinegger, Chief Executive,
Lombard International Assurance S.A, Luxembourg.

"A brilliant, gifted, genuine and inspiring motivational trainer - check him out - highly recommended."
Barefoot Doctor, International Speaker
and Author of the internationally acclaimed
"HANDBOOK FOR THE URBAN WARRIOR"
and many other titles. http://www.barefootdoctorworld.com

"My first encounter with you gave me the signal that you are something special. Your way of presenting is unique. You are provoking your attendees to dig into themselves as most of the tools for our success are within ourselves. Your seminar opened new windows in my mind. Many positive changes occurred in my life in the last years and I can say your contribution was the catalyst."
Miha Kovacic, Manager,
Slovenia Convention Centre

Bibliography

http://edcorner.stanford.edu/authorMaterialInfo.html?topicId=7&mid=215

Strategies for Growth by Chris Zook and Jimmy Allen www.bain.com

Technical Assistance Research Programme, U.S.A

Zero Defections Harvard Business Review - Reichard & Sasser

http://wpcarey.asu.edu/csl/2004-National-Customer-Rage-Study.cfm

Technical Assistance Research Programme, U.S.A.

www.ritzcarlton.com

Technical Assistance Research Programme, U.S.A

Article by Janet Adamy, Wall Street Journal April 2006

http://www.innovations-report.com/html/reports/social_sciences/
   report-13848.htm

Yankelovich, October 2006

'Guerrilla Marketing' by Jay Conrad Levinson

http://www.medtronic.com/employment/

The Future of Competition, Harvard Business School Press, 2004

www.sonystyle.com

www.adidas.com

Albert Mehrabian's 7-38-55 Rule

http://psychologytoday.com/articles/pto-20021209-000001.html

http://www.apa.org/monitor/sep98/world.html

en.wikipedia.org/wiki/Toyota

http://www.time.com/time/magazine/article/0,9171,1808633,00.html

http://www.nasscom.in/Nasscom/templates/NormalPage.aspx?id=53345

http://www.watsonwyatt.com/europe/ireland/

Gallup Q12 Benchmarking Survey

Gallup Management Journal

http://edition.cnn.com/2004/BUSINESS/05/09/go.sleep.office/index.html

http://www.cfo.com/article.cfm/l_comments/10610786?context_id=2984789#3155

Article by Andy Serwer, Fortune Magazine March 7 2005

http://strategic-hcm.blogspot.com/2008/01/best-companies-for-leaders.html

Fortune Magazine, Top 0 Companies for Leaders 2007 http://money.cnn.com/galleries/
   2007/fortune/0709/gallery.leaders_global_topten.fortune/3.html

http://strategic-hcm.blogspot.com/2008/0/best-companies-for-leaders.html

http://www.ibm.com/ibm/sjp/

Fortune Magazine, Top 0 Companies for Leaders 2007 http://money.cnn.com/galleries/
   2007/fortune/0709/gallery.leaders_global_topten.fortune/3.html

http://www.000ventures.com/business_guide/crosscuttings/shared_values.html

http://www.leader-values.com/Content/detail.asp?ContentDetailID=950

www.sfa.ie ISAWorker Mobility Report 2007

http://hays.com.au/news

http://www.timberland.com/corp/index.jsp?page=pressrelease&eid=850002702

http://www.essex.ac.uk/news/2004/nr20040924b.htm

Learning and Skills Council (LSC). The Success Report 2004

http://money.cnn.com/magazines/fortune/bestcompanies/2008/snapshots/.html

http://www.som.cranfield.ac.uk/som/news/story.asp?id=390

http://www.management-issues.com/2007/8/22/research/the-key-to-commitment.asp

https://www.vitalfriends.com/library/pdf/VitalFriendsMediaKit.pdf

http://smaartadvice.com/articles/saart0000.php

http://www.apa.org/journals/releases/bul36803.pdf

http://www.usatoday.com/money/industries/technology/maney/2004-03-0-money_x.htm

http://www.umich.edu/news/index.html?rel

http://resources.greatplacetowork.com/article/pdf/final_2006_conference_sharp_
    keynote_transcript_90406.pd

http://www.fastcompany.com/magazine/04/hiring.html?page=0%2C'

www.ritzcarlton.com

www.goldcorp.inc

http://www.maclife.com/article/exclusive_a_day_in_the_life_of_an_apple_genius

Breakpoint and Beyond

http://www.sciencedaily.com/releases/2003/02/03020407425.htm

 (Presentation delivered at Stanford University June 2006)

http://www.about-nokia.com/history/

http://www.london.edu/assets/documents/PDF/GEM_Annual_Report_v0.pdf

www.nesta.org.uk

http://en.wikipedia.org/wiki/Failure

http://money.cnn.com/magazines/fortune/globalmostadmired/top50/

http://www.fastcompany.com/magazine/89/creativity.html

http://www.bbc.co.uk/pressoffice/pressreleases/stoes/2003/0_october/05/mind_
    millionaire.shtml

http://entrepreneurship.mit.edu

http://gmj.gallup.com/content/296/Big-Impact-Small-Interactions.aspx happy

www.kevinkellyunlimited.com

http://www.futurepundit.com/archives/002945.html

http://www.thecrimson.com/article.aspx?ref=508644l